SUPER STEM

A Day at Work with a
MOLECULAR
BIOLOGIST

ALANA OLSEN

PowerKiDS
press™

New York

Published in 2016 by The Rosen Publishing Group, Inc.
29 East 21st Street, New York, NY 10010

First Edition

Editor: Caitie McAneney
Book Design: Katelyn Heinle

Photo Credits: Cover Christopher Futcher/E+/Getty Images; cover, pp. 1, 3, 4, 6–8, 10–14, 16, 18, 20, 22–24 (molecular vector design) phloxii/Shutterstock.com; p. 5 (top) wavebreakmedia/Shutterstock.com; p. 5 (bottom) Michal Kowalski/Shutterstock.com; p. 7 snapgalleria/Shutterstock.com; p. 9 Monkey Business Images/Shutterstock.com; p. 11 (main) Nicolas Loran/E+/Getty Images; p. 11 (inset) Filip Ristevski/Shutterstock.com; p. 12 Baloncici/Shutterstock.com; p. 13 Monty Rakusen/Cultura/Getty Images; p. 15 Gordon Bell/Shutterstock.com; p. 17 (top) Minerva Studio/Shutterstock.com; p. 17 (bottom) Dragon Images/Shutterstock.com; p. 19 (top) photofriday/Shutterstock.com; p. 19 (bottom) Peopleimages/E+/Getty Images; p. 20 Ramona Heim/Shutterstock.com; p. 21 DAN DUNKLEY/Science Photo Library/Getty Images; p. 22 Jacek Chabraszewski/Shutterstock.com.

Library of Congress Cataloging-in-Publication Data

Olsen, Alana, author.
 A day at work with a molecular biologist / Alana Olsen.
    pages cm. — (Super STEM careers)
 Includes index.
 ISBN 978-1-5081-4410-6 (pbk.)
 ISBN 978-1-5081-4411-3 (6 pack)
 ISBN 978-1-5081-4412-0 (library binding)
 1. Molecular biology—Vocational guidance—Juvenile literature. 2. Molecular biologists—Juvenile literature. I. Title.
 QH506.O47 2016
 572.8023—dc23
                              2015027364

Manufactured in the United States of America

CPSIA Compliance Information: Batch #BW16PK: For Further Information contact Rosen Publishing, New York, New York at 1-800-237-9932

CONTENTS

STUDYING THE SMALL THINGS

Every living thing in this world—from flowers to fish to people—is made of cells. They're the building blocks of the living world. You can't see cells—they're far too small. However, they hold the key to important advances in medicine, **technology**, farming, and many other fields.

Molecular biologists are scientists who study **molecules** and cells. They work in labs, using strong microscopes to take a look at how cells work, grow, and change. A career in molecular biology combines chemistry and biology. It's a great example of STEM, which stands for "science, technology, **engineering**, and math."

SUPER STEM SMARTS

Molecular biologists often study bacteria cultures in petri dishes. This is an easy way to make bacteria colonies grow so they can be studied with a microscope.

Although molecular biology is a **complex** field in many ways, it involves studying the simplest parts of living organisms.

WHAT IS MOLECULAR BIOLOGY?

Molecular biologists use science every day. They especially use biology, which is the study of living things. Molecular biology is concerned with the structure of cells and how they work at the molecular level. Cells grow and multiply over time, and they can also change with the conditions around them.

Different kinds of cells do different things. Some tiny organisms, such as bacteria, are made up of a single, simple cell. Larger organisms, such as plants and animals, are made up of many larger and more complex cells. Cells are made up of different parts, and each part has an important job.

Molecular biologists have to understand each part of a cell. This picture shows a human cell and some of its most important parts.

PARTS OF THE HUMAN CELL

CYTOPLASM: liquid matter that fills the cell and is mostly water

LYSOSOMES: break down large molecules into smaller pieces the cell can use

MEMBRANE: outer boundary of the cell, which lets some matter in and keeps other matter out

MITOCHONDRIA: create energy

NUCLEUS: "brain" of the cell, tells the cell what to do

RIBOSOMES: "factories" that make **proteins** for the cell

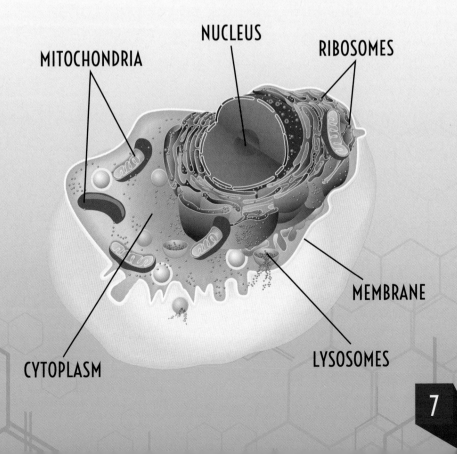

A CLOSE LOOK AT DNA

DNA is like an instruction manual for all the cells in your body. Each person has different DNA, and that's what makes us look and act differently. DNA is made up of two chains of molecules that are twisted together. It's found in the nucleus of an organism's cells. DNA tells the cells to make different proteins.

DNA makes up our genes. A gene is a piece of DNA that works as the code for a certain protein in the body. Genes are passed down from both parents, so offspring often resemble one or both parents. However, the genes from two parents are very different.

The study of genes is called genetics. Some molecular biologists focus on genetics. They can look at a person's DNA to see if the code for a certain disease, or illness, is in their cells.

TECHNOLOGY ON THE JOB

Molecular biologists spend most of their time in a lab with special technology that helps them do their job. They use small, simple tools, as well as some of the most advanced laboratory tools available.

A common tool found in a molecular biology lab is a petri dish. Petri dishes hold small samples, such as a blood sample. Molecular biologists can put a petri dish under a microscope to magnify its contents. Then, they can examine, or observe, the cells within the sample. Molecular biologists use microscopes that are very strong so they can examine cell structures that are very tiny.

SUPER STEM SMARTS

Some microscopes have a built-in camera. The camera may connect to a computer, so biologists can study the image on a computer screen.

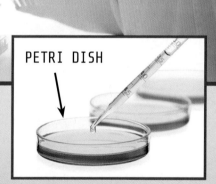

PETRI DISH

Molecular biologists also put samples on special plates called microplates. They put the microplates into a microplate reader to get a clear picture of the cells that make up the sample.

Molecular biologists work with samples that can be very **sensitive**. They need to be kept at a certain temperature or in certain lighting. Because of that, some biology labs have cold rooms and dark rooms. Some have a deep freezer that stores bacteria cultures at very low temperatures. Molecular biologists also use water baths, which surround a vessel with water that's at a certain temperature.

A refrigerated centrifuge is a tool that separates two liquids or two solids suspended in a liquid, which is useful in analyzing samples. Incubators create the right conditions for bacteria and cells to grow.

AUTOCLAVE

SUPER STEM SMARTS
An autoclave is a tool that **sterilizes** samples using steam and pressure.

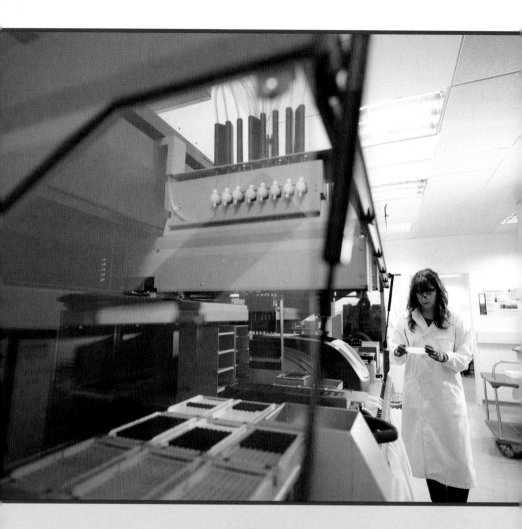

DNA sequencers are machines that tell molecular biologists important information about DNA samples.

MOLECULAR BIOLOGY AND ENGINEERING

Some molecular biologists aren't interested only in **analyzing** cells and DNA. They take what they know of molecular structures and work on creating something new. That's a kind of engineering.

Molecular biologists who work in **industry** use their knowledge of molecules to **develop** methods to use, make, and store medicines, chemicals, and food. Some work in biotechnological manufacturing, which involves using living systems and organisms to make products. These molecular biologists may find a job with the Food and Drug Administration (FDA) or the U.S. Department of Agriculture. Some work for food and drink suppliers that are interested in creating new products.

Some molecular biologists genetically engineer crops that can't be killed by disease or changes in their surroundings.

MANUFACTURING MEDICINES

Molecular biologists play a very important part in society because they examine how medicines and drugs affect people. They also come up with new medicines and drugs to help people. They might work in the pharmaceutical field, which is concerned with developing and giving out the right medicines to treat certain illnesses.

A molecular biologist might also look at how diseases affect the human body. They can look at blood and waste from a person to see how a disease affects their body on the molecular level. They may also see how a medicine is affecting a person by analyzing their blood and waste after they've taken medicine.

SUPER STEM SMARTS

Molecular biologists interested in medicine might work for pharmaceutical companies, hospital, clinics, or even for the U.S. Department of Health and Human Services.

Some molecular biologists are involved with developing and manufacturing vaccines, which are drugs that prepare a person's body to fight an illness before it starts.

MOLECULAR MATH

Math skills are very important if you want to become a molecular biologist. Geometry is the mathematical study of lines, angles, surfaces, and solids. The shape of molecules is very important when identifying them and guessing what they might do.

Statistics is an area of math concerned with collecting and analyzing numbers, or numerical data, to find patterns and make **inferences**. This helps molecular biologists see which genes are most commonly active in people with certain features or diseases. A molecular biologist may find that every time a certain gene is active, a person is more at risk for developing a disease.

Molecular biologists use statistics to find exact links between genes and disease. In the future, they might be able to do gene therapy, which means fixing the genes in a person's cells to treat disease.

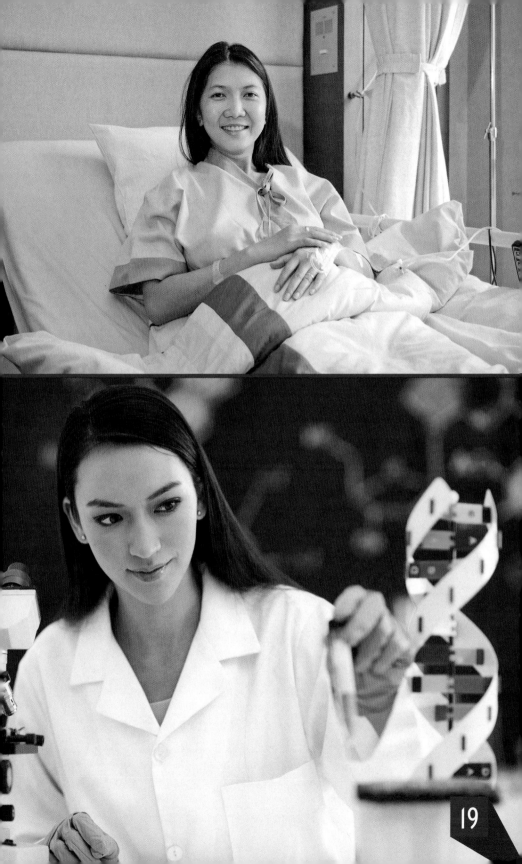

All molecular biologists examine, analyze, and make inferences about the molecular structure of living things. However, a day at work with a molecular biologist depends on what field they work in.

Some molecular biologists work in agriculture or environmental science. They examine living things in nature and on farms, and see how they're affected by pollution, pests, temperature, and other changes in the environment. Some work in food processing to genetically modify, or change, food to be healthier and last longer. Some may even

work on criminal cases. They can examine samples from a crime scene and match them to a person's DNA.

SUPER STEM SMARTS

Some molecular biologists look at how certain chemicals negatively affect living things. This is called toxicology.

Virologists are molecular biologists who study viruses and how they affect a person's body.

BECOMING A MOLECULAR BIOLOGIST

Does a career as a molecular biologist sound exciting? If so, you can start preparing for a career right away. Pay special attention in your science and math classes, and take as many STEM classes as you can in high school.

Molecular biologists need a bachelor's degree in biology, chemistry, or a related field. Some people earn their master's degree or Ph.D. in molecular biology or a related area of study to advance their careers.

Molecular biologists are masters at studying the smallest pieces of living things. They know that inside each cell and strand of DNA there's a promise for a better future.

GLOSSARY

analyze: To study something deeply.

complex: Not easy to understand or explain.

develop: To work on something over time. Also, to become sick with an illness.

engineering: The use of science and math to build better objects.

industry: A group of businesses that provide a certain product or service.

inference: A conclusion or opinion that's formed because of known facts or evidence.

molecule: The smallest possible amount of something that has all the characteristics of that thing.

protein: A long chain of structural matter made by the body that helps a cell perform major functions.

sensitive: Easily harmed or damaged by certain conditions.

sterilize: To clean something by destroying germs or bacteria.

technology: The way people do something using tools and the tools that they use.

INDEX

WEBSITES

Due to the changing nature of Internet links, PowerKids Press has developed an online list of websites related to the subject of this book. This site is updated regularly. Please use this link to access the list: www.powerkidslinks.com/ssc/mbio